To:

_____

From:

_____

D0326701

sassy & sophisticated

published by DaySpring Cards, Inc. Siloam Springs, AR 72761
www.dayspring.com

December 31

$\mathcal{K}$eep traveling steadily along HIS pathway and IN due season HE will honor you with every blessing.   PSALM 37:34

January 1

God knows how to pack the good stuff into our day, our week, our year—even if our attitude gets a little wrinkled at times.

January 2

*G*ive your cares to god—He loves you like crazy!

December 30

*A*bove all else, guard your affections. For they influence everything else in your life. PROVERBS 4:23

January 3

*L*et Him have all your worries and cares, for He is always thinking about you and watching everything that concerns you.   I PETER 5:7

December 29

*S*he was comfortable in her own shoes, and she discovered they looked best with the uniqueness God had given her.

January 4

There's more happiness in a single moment of God's presence than in anything else in life (and He doesn't mind if you sweeten the happy moments with a little chocolate).

December 28

*A*ll who humble themselves before the Lord shall be given every blessing, and shall have wonderful peace. PSALM 37:11

January 5

You have let me experience the joys of life and the exquisite pleasures of Your own eternal presence.   PSALM 16:11

December 27

_S_he is a woman of strength and dignity, and has no fear of old age.

PROVERBS 31:25

January 6

*G*o after your dreams—God created you to live them!

December 26

It was time to put on a new hat—
the one stitched together with hope and courage.

January 7

When dreams come true at last, there is life and joy.   PROVERBS 13:12

December 25

*T*hese will be his royal titles:

"wonderful," "counselor,"

"the mighty god,"

"the everlasting father,"

"the prince of peace."   ISAIAH 9:6

January 8

She loved the LORD with all her heart, and it cast an amazing light on everything she did.

December 24

I bring you the most joyful news ever announced...
the savior—yes, the messiah, the lord—has been born.

LUKE 2:10, 11

January 9

God looked over all that He had made, and it was excellent in every way. GENESIS 1:31

December 23

Miracles are God's way of showing us that if we believe,
all things are possible.

*J*anuary 10

*E*very woman should have a mirror that reflects her spirit—that's where God brings out her true beauty.

December 22

*G*od HIMSELF is blessing you forever.   PSALM 45:2

January 11

*B*e beautiful inside, in your hearts, with the lasting charm of a gentle and quiet spirit that is so precious to God.   I PETER 3:4

December 21

$\mathcal{F}$ill all who love you with your happiness.   PSALM 5:11

January 12

She welcomes the years with arms open wide and loves life with the kind of passion that comes straight from God.

December 20

God celebrates you every day of the year.

January 13

Rejoice in every day of life.   ECCLESIASTES 11:8

December 19

I will sing to the Lord because He has blessed me so richly.

PSALM 13:6

January 14

The good things god has for you are more exciting than a clearance shoe sale and a box of chocolates put together.

December 13

I am always thinking of the LORD... Heart, body and soul are filled with joy.   PSALM 16:8, 9

January 15

$\mathcal{T}$he LORD will guide you continually, and satisfy you with all good things.   ISAIAH 58:11

December 17

*J*oy is the soul's celebration of everything God has done.

*J*anuary 16

*B*e inspired. Be brave. Be you!

December 16

Let us walk in the light of the Lord.   ISAIAH 2:5

January 17

𝒴our workmanship is marvelous—and how well I know it. You were there while I was being formed in utter seclusion!

PSALM 139:14, 15

December 15

Let your good deeds glow for all to see, so that they will praise your heavenly father.   MATTHEW 5:16

January 18

*S*he LIVES. she LOVES. she LAUGHS. she makes every day a celebration of who she is in christ.

December 14

She was absolutely glowing in her fashionable red dress, sparkly earrings, and passion for god.

January 19

Because of what christ has done, we have become gifts to god that He delights in.   EPHESIANS 1:11

December 13

God's son shines out with god's glory.   HEBREWS 1:3

January 20

*B*e fabulous—God spared no enthusiasm when He created you!

December 12

Where is the newborn king?... for we have seen his star... and have come to worship him.   MATTHEW 2:2

January 21

Thank you for making me so wonderfully complex!
it is amazing to think about.   PSALM 139:14

December 11

She loved to gaze at the stars in the sky, for they gleamed with the majesty of the one who created them.

January 22

She's the kind of person who looks at a cloud and says to herself, "There's a rainbow coming in just a little while." Then she kicks off her shoes and dances in the puddles until the sun comes out again.

December 10

$\mathcal{I}$ am on my way to heaven; I belong to christ.   I JOHN 2:4

January 23

"*For* I know the plans I have for you," says the LORD. "They are plans for good."   JEREMIAH 29:11

December 9

Miracles happen...joy strengthens...love conquers all!

January 24

No doubt about it—a woman on fire for God
is a force to be reckoned with.

December 8

*O*ur light is from Your light. Pour out Your unfailing love on those who know You!   PSALM 36:9, 10

January 25

*L*ove the Lord and follow His plan for your lives. cling to Him and serve Him enthusiastically.   JOSHUA 22:5

December 7

*H*er heart believed... and she sparkled from head to toe.

January 26

*I*n hard times she had learned three things—she was stronger than she ever imagined, Jesus was closer than she ever realized, and she was loved more than she ever knew.

December 6

He sends the snow in all its lovely whiteness, and scatters the frost upon the ground.   PSALM 147:16

January 27

*G*od loves you very much...don't be afraid! calm yourself; be strong—yes, strong! DANIEL 10:19

December 5

Decorate your life with God's love.

January 28

*H*er spirit loved to bask in the brightness of her future.

December 4

$\mathscr{E}$verything comes from god alone.   ROMANS 11:36

January 29

A bright future lies ahead!   PROVERBS 24:14

December 3

Through christ, all the kindness of god has been poured out upon us.   ROMANS 1:5

January 30

A woman of enthusiasm is glorious to see–and glorious to be!

December 2

The most fashionable coat we will ever wear is one made of kindness and love.

January 31

Work hard and cheerfully at all you do, just as though you were working for the Lord. COLOSSIANS 3:23

December 1

God showed HIS great love for us by sending christ.   ROMANS 5:8

February 1

The godly woman faces her challenges with prayer, a sense of adventure, and a great pair of boots.

November 30

Amazing Thought #37: You are loved and cared for every moment by the God who holds the universe in His hands.

February 2

$\mathcal{W}$hat a wonderful God we have—He is the Father of our Lord Jesus Christ, the source of every mercy.   II CORINTHIANS 1:3, 4

November 29

Sing praises to the Lord! Raise your voice in song to Him who rides upon the clouds.   PSALM 68:4

February 3

$\mathcal{A}$ wise woman will always ask for directions—
and God will always give them.

November 28

*Y*our power and goodness, Lord, reach to the highest heavens. You have done such wonderful things. PSALM 71:19

February 4

If you want to know what God wants you to do, ask Him, and He will gladly tell you.   JAMES 1:5

November 27

Lord, let my life be a continual melody of thankfulness to you!

February 5

*T*he best form of exercise has nothing to do with equipment—
and everything to do with faith.

November 26

How we thank you, Lord! Your mighty miracles give proof that you care.   PSALM 75:1

February 6

Spend your time and energy in the exercise of keeping spiritually fit. I TIMOTHY 4:7

November 25

Come before HIM with thankful hearts. PSALM 95:2

February 7

Trials build patience, make us strong, and teach us that sometimes prayer and truffles do go together.

November 24

*B*eing thankful is a wonderful way to fill our hearts with joy.

February 8

When your patience is finally in full bloom, then you will be ready for anything, strong in character, full and complete. JAMES 1:4

November 23

When she speaks, her words are wise, and kindness is the rule for everything she says.   PROVERBS 31:26

February 9

When God asks you to step out of your comfort zone, *do it*— and wear a glorious pair of shoes.

November 22

Those who use god's wisdom are safe.   PROVERBS 28:26

February 10

When I am afraid, I will put my confidence in you.   PSALM 56:3

November 21

The woman who loves wisdom is elegant beyond compare.

February 11

$\mathcal{G}$od wants to use you to adorn the world with HIS beauty—
no matter what kind of hair day you're having!

November 20

$\mathcal{A}$lways be thankful. COLOSSIANS 3:15

February 12

May you always be doing those good, kind things that show you are a child of god. **PHILIPPIANS 1:11**

November 19

Remind each other of God's goodness and be thankful.

EPHESIANS 5:4

February 13

Hope! it will keep you looking incredibly young.

November 18

$\int$he thought about everything she wanted to say to God, and it always started with, "Thank you."

February 14

Hope will keep you happy and full of peace. ROMANS 15:13

November 17

Your own soul is nourished when you are kind. PROVERBS 11:17

February 15

$\mathcal{G}$od saw to every detail, and her character grew more and more beautiful.

November 16

May my spoken words and unspoken thoughts be pleasing even to you, o Lord.   PSALM 19:14

February 16

Lord, you are our Father. we are the clay and you are the Potter. we are all formed by your hand.   ISAIAH 64:8

November 15

Words are such important things to be careful with.

February 17

Hold tightly to your faith, even when there's no chocolate in sight.

November 14

He is like a father to us, tender and sympathetic.   PSALM 103:13

February 18

What is faith? It is the confident assurance that something we want is going to happen.   HEBREWS 11:1

November 13

The lovingkindness of the Lord is from everlasting to everlasting.

PSALM 103:17

February 19

$\mathcal{P}$ut on comfortable shoes and head in the direction of your dreams—God has prepared the path ahead of you.

November 12

God loves you no matter what.

February 20

*B*e strong! Be courageous! Do not be afraid...! For the Lord your God will be with you.   DEUTERONOMY 31:6

November 11

*H*e is the god who keeps every promise. PSALM 146:6

February 21

Joy is strength, and laughter is a little pick-me-up for the soul.

November 10

Head up, shoulders back, thoughts positive, heart set on the promises of God.

February 22

The joy of the LORD is your strength.   NEHEMIAH 8:10

November 9

Trust the Lord completely.   PROVERBS 3:5

February 23

We can do great things if we focus on the great God who created us!

November 8

𝒢od, who knows all hearts, knows yours.   PROVERBS 24:12

February 24

The people who know their god shall be strong and do great things.

DANIEL 11:32

November 7

The heart is a fragile thing, it can't be trusted to just anyone. Thank goodness God isn't just anyone.

February 25

Make the most of the opportunities God gives you to shine today.

November 6

*I*n everything you do, put god first, and He will direct you.

PROVERBS 3:6

February 26

$\mathcal{T}$hose who are wise—the people of God—shall shine as brightly as the sun's brilliance.   DANIEL 12:3

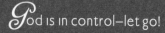

November 5

God is in control—let go!

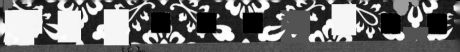

February 27

Who needs a facelift when god's word can renew the spirit, soul, and body!

November 4

How great he is! His power is absolute! His understanding is unlimited. PSALM 147:5

February 28

*Y*ou have been chosen by god who has given you this new kind of life. COLOSSIANS 3:12

November 3

𝒴ou are merciful and gentle, Lord, slow in getting angry, full of constant lovingkindness.   PSALM 86:15

February 29

*T*aking a leap of faith is like buying a pair of shoes you have nothing to go with—it's always worth it.

November 2

With such an enormous amount of stuff to be learned, there are a million reasons to thank God for being patient with us.

March 1

*T*hese trials are only to test your faith, to see whether or not
it is strong and pure.   1 PETER 1:7

November 1

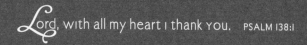 *Lord,* with all my heart I thank you.   PSALM 138:1

March 2

*T*oday's beauty secret: contentment—it's great for the soul's complexion.

October 31

The good shall never lose God's blessing. PROVERBS 10:30

March 3

I have learned the secret of contentment in every situation.

PHILIPPIANS 4:12

October 30

*Y*our gifts are beyond compare...and with god, your dreams are always within reach.

March 4

A girl can never have too many pairs of shoes, or too many reasons to thank god.

October 29

I will bless the Lord and not forget the glorious things He does for me.   PSALM 103:2

March 5

My constant boast is God. I can never thank you enough!

PSALM 44:8

October 28

When you let your heart receive god's love, infinite blessings come with it!

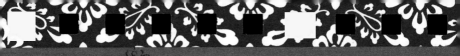

March 6

She knew joy was one of her best accessories, so she made up her mind to wear it every day.

October 27

$\mathcal{T}$here is nothing but goodness in Him!   PSALM 92:15

March 7

A happy face means a glad heart. PROVERBS 15:13

October 26

God is at work within you.   PHILIPPIANS 2:13

March 8

*C*hocolate, sweet chocolate...
let us never abandon the things god has given us to enjoy.

October 25

God's love can be seen in every circumstance.

March 9

*T*rust should be in the living God who always richly gives us all we need for our enjoyment.   I TIMOTHY 6:17

October 24

May God who gives patience, steadiness, and encouragement help you live in complete harmony.   ROMANS 15:5

March 10

Everything comes from god alone. ROMANS II:36

October 23

May you be given more and more of God's kindness, peace, and love.   JUDE 1:2

March 11

She started her day with a simple prayer, "Lord, lead the way." Then she stepped out the door with a heart full of courage.

October 22

The sweetest thing God adds to life is the gift of a trusted friend.

March 12

Let me see your kindness to me in the morning, for I am trusting you. show me where to walk, for my prayer is sincere.   PSALM 143:8

October 21

Thank you, Lord! How good you are! Your love for us continues on forever.   PSALM 106:1

March 13

Love never goes out of style.

October 20

I will always trust in you and in your mercy.   PSALM 13:5

March 14

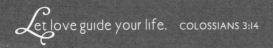

Let love guide your life.   COLOSSIANS 3:14

October 19

Lord, put my feet on the path you've chosen for me, and let my heart be content.

March 15

*I*f we believe we can change the world, God will show us how to do it!

October 18

All God's words are right, and everything He does is worthy of our trust.   PSALM 33:4

March 16

You can get anything—anything you ask for in prayer— if you believe. MATTHEW 21:22

October 17

Joy rises in my heart until I burst out in songs of praise to Him.

PSALM 28:7

March 17

A shoe sale is a great mood-lifter…but it takes a good prayer to lift the spirit.

October 16

Refresh your soul with hope—let your spirit be filled with joy!

March 18

Lord, you are my shield, my glory, and my only hope.
You alone can lift my head. PSALM 3:3

October 15

*E*very path ʜᴇ guides us on ɪs fragrant with ʜɪs lovingkindness.   ᴘsᴀʟᴍ 25:10

March 19

*D*ay planners are great for organizing our days…
but god is the only one who can organize our life.

October 14

You alone are my god. My times are in your hands.   PSALM 31:14

March 20

*Y*ou saw me before I was born and scheduled each day of my life before I began to breathe.   PSALM 139:16

October 13

Let your day rest in god's hand, and enjoy wherever it takes you!

March 21

𝒯he LORD will work out HIS plans for my life—
for your loving-kindness, LORD, continues forever.

PSALM 138:8

October 12

We know how dearly god loves us, and we feel HIS warm love everywhere. ROMANS 5:5

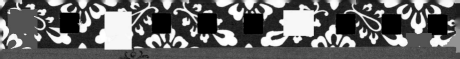

March 22

There is radiance in a woman who knows how priceless she is to God.

October 11

𝒴our steadfast love, O LORD, is as great as all the heavens.
Your faithfulness reaches beyond the clouds.   PSALM 36:5

March 23

You are precious to me and honored, and I love you.   ISAIAH 43:4

October 10

*B*eing trendy is fun, she thought, but there was an incredible comfort in knowing God's love for her would never change.

March 24

$\mathcal{A}$ woman who fears and reverences God shall be greatly praised.   PROVERBS 31:30

October 9

My protection and success come from God alone.   PSALM 62:7

March 25

If you can pray, you can conquer!

October 8

Whatever god says to us is full of living power.   HEBREWS 4:12

March 26

When I pray, you answer me and encourage me by giving me the strength I need.   PSALM 138:3

October 7

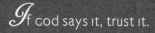

If God says it, trust it.

March 27

She looked up and knew everything was going to be more than o.k.– it was going to work out perfectly.

October 6

*B*e delighted with the Lord. Then He will give you all your heart's desires.   PSALM 37:4

March 28

Each morning I will look to you in heaven and lay my requests before you. PSALM 5:3

October 5

Just tell me what to do and I will do it, Lord. As long as I live I'll wholeheartedly obey.   PSALM 119:33, 34

March 29

God created every soul to sing.

October 4

She wanted to grow in beauty and grace, so she asked God
to show her the seeds she should plant in the soil of her heart.

March 30

I SING HIS songs and pray to GOD who gives me life. PSALM 42:8

October 3

He is the strength of my heart; He is mine forever! PSALM 73:26

March 31

*H*appy are those who are strong in the LORD, who want above all else to follow your steps.   PSALM 84:5

October 2

She was full of joy and generosity, and everyone knew her heart belonged to God.

April 1

A woman armed with chocolate and a prayer partner needs little else to get through the day.

October 1

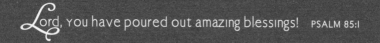

Lord, you have poured out amazing blessings!   PSALM 85:1

April 2

If two of you agree down here on earth concerning anything you ask for, my Father in heaven will do it for you.   MATTHEW 18:19

September 30

Life is adorned with the beauty of god's blessings.

April 3

You are bright and gifted—you are a woman of God.

September 29

*G*od blesses those who obey him.   PROVERBS 16:20

April 4

𝒴our greatest glory will be that you belong to HIM.

II THESSALONIANS 1:12

September 28

We can make our plans, but the final outcome is in God's hands.

PROVERBS 16:1

April 5

*W*isdom in three words: *L*ord help me!

September 27

Open your heart to God, and life will open the doors to your dreams.

April 6

In my distress I screamed to the Lord for his help. And he heard me from heaven. PSALM 18:6

September 26

If you search for good, you will find God's favor.   PROVERBS 11:27

April 7

I can multi-task if that means having dessert and a salad at the same time.

September 25

Do you want to be truly rich? You already are if you are happy and good.   *1 TIMOTHY 6:6*

April 8

A cheerful heart does good like medicine. PROVERBS 17:22

September 24

*S*he knew the day would bring opportunities to make God smile, and she would happily take each one of them.

April 9

The LORD will give you an abundance of good things.

DEUTERONOMY 28:11

September 23

*W*isdom is a fountain of life. PROVERBS 16:22

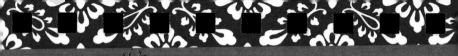

April 10

*I*t really is all about love. god says so.

September 22

I will praise the LORD no matter what happens. I will constantly speak of HIS glories and grace.   PSALM 34:1

April 11

$\mathcal{P}$ay all your debts except the debt of love for others—
never finish paying that! ROMANS 13:8

September 21

There are some days when you just have to hang the 'be brave' sign on your heart and dive in!

April 12

Love the LORD your God with all your heart, soul, and mind.

MATTHEW 22:37

September 20

*E*very morning tell Him, "Thank you for your kindness," and every evening rejoice in all His faithfulness. PSALM 92:2

April 13

Sit quietly. Breathe deeply. Hope steadily. God is working on your behalf this very moment.

September 19

He is good to everyone, and HIS compassion is intertwined with everything He does.   PSALM 145:9

April 14

My God is changeless in His love for me, and He will come and help me.   PSALM 59:10

September 18

Life will have its cloudy days. I think god knew it was the best way for our hearts to truly appreciate the sunshine.

April 15

I will tell everyone how good you are, and of your constant, daily care. I walk in the strength of the Lord.   PSALM 71:15, 16

September 17

Love each other just as much as I love you.   JOHN 13:34

April 16

God told her anything is possible, so she lived her life believing it with all her heart.

September 16

May your roots go down deep into the soil of god's marvelous love. EPHESIANS 3:17

April 17

With god everything is possible.   MARK 10:27

September 15

Life is all about loving god and loving others—
it really is as simple as that.

April 18

You love me so much! *You* are constantly so kind!   PSALM 86:13

September 14

When the Holy Spirit controls our lives He will produce this kind of fruit in us: love, joy, peace, patience, kindness, goodness, faithfulness, gentleness and self-control.   GALATIANS 5:22, 23

April 19

Be good to yourself. god only made one of you!

September 13

Moods have a way of swinging
just when you need them to hold still–
and there's one word for that: *pray*.

April 20

*T*urn to HIM SO HE can... send you wonderful times of refreshment from the presence of the LORD.   ACTS 3:19

September 12

Lord... I am looking up to you in constant hope.   PSALM 86:3

April 21

I refresh the humble and give new courage to those with repentant hearts. ISAIAH 57:15

September 11

I will meditate about your glory, splendor, majesty and miracles.

PSALM 145:5

April 22

A great day of shopping is sublime...

quiet time with god, divine.

September 10

A great pair of heels can't solve everything...
but they do lift you a teensy bit closer to God.

April 23

You have let me experience the joys of life and the exquisite pleasures of your own eternal presence.   PSALM 16:11

September 9

Happy are all who search for god, and always do his will.

PSALM 119:2

April 24

Friendship with god is reserved for those who reverence Him. with them alone He shares the secrets of His promises.   PSALM 25:14

September 8

*B*e happy. grow in christ. live in harmony and peace.

II CORINTHIANS 13:11

April 25

She knew there would be bumps in the road, so she protected her heart, adjusted her attitude, and held onto God's promises with both hands.

September 7

There's a lot to be said about choosing happiness—
and it's best to remember...it is a choice!

April 26

He will shield you with HIS wings! THey will shelter you.
HIS faithful promises are your armor.   PSALM 91:4

September 6

Pray all the time. EPHESIANS 6:18

April 27

*O*pen your arms wide and let god bless you!

September 5

*T*alk with each other much about the LORD. EPHESIANS 5:19

April 28

$\mathcal{Y}$ou will receive every blessing you can use! PSALM 81:10

September 4

Live. Laugh. Love. Pray.
PRAISE. Every day!

April 29

Those who trust the LORD shall be given every blessing.   PSALM 37:9

September 3

All who fear HIM are blessed beyond expression.　PSALM 112:1

April 30

God likes to spoil us with His blessings. He doesn't mind the occasional spoiling of ourselves either.

September 2

If we're going to be enthusiastic about life, we must be passionate about God.

May 1

$\mathcal{G}$od cares about everything in your life because He cares so much about you.

September 1

We meditate upon your kindness and your love. PSALM 48:9

May 2

*Y*ou have always cared for me.   PSALM 4:1

August 31

In silence and stillness, your spirit can dream.

May 3

When we are kind, God smiles.

August 30

Wisdom and truth will enter the very center of your being, filling your life with joy. PROVERBS 2:10

May 4

Honor goes to kind and gracious women.   PROVERBS 11:16

August 29

O God, my heart is quiet and confident. PSALM 57:7

May 5

Anytime is a good time for a quiet prayer...
or dark chocolate.

August 28

ℋer attitude was as light-as-air—
she had given god all her care.

May 6

There is a right time for everything.   ECCLESIASTES 3:1

August 27

Help me to do your will, for you are my God. Lead me in good paths, for your spirit is good. PSALM 143:10

May 7

Make room in your closet for a fun pair of shoes—and room in your day to show someone God's love.

August 26

You are gifted—and God used the infinite resources of His goodness to create you.

May 8

If I had the gift of faith so that I could speak to a mountain and make it move, I would still be worth nothing at all without love.

1 CORINTHIANS 13:2

August 25

What can we ever say to such wonderful things as these?
If God is on our side, who can ever be against us?   ROMANS 8:31

May 9

*T*ake a moment today to think about something wonderful God has done for you.

August 24

Work hard and with gladness all the time... doing the will of god with all your hearts. EPHESIANS 6:7

May 10

Let all the joys of the godly well up in praise to the Lord.   PSALM 33:1

August 23

*P*ut your heart into *everything*—and see what God will do through you.

May 11

*D*on't hold back a kind word or a loving deed—
they have God's blessing all over them!

August 22

You are good and do only good; make me follow your lead.

PSALM 119:68

May 12

$\mathcal{D}$ay by day the Lord observes the good deeds done by godly men, and gives them eternal rewards.   PSALM 37:18

August 21

Kick off your shoes and dance through your day—
God will happily take the lead.

May 13

The growth of our faith is a journey—and a little chocolate helps along the way.

August 20

The Lord makes us strong!   PSALM 81:1

May 14

I will praise the LORD no matter what happens.   PSALM 34:1

August 19

*C*heer up! Take courage if you are depending on the Lord.

PSALM 31:24

May 15

The best way to end a meal is with dessert...
and a day with prayer.

August 18

She put on her rose-colored glasses and looked at everything through the eyes of faith—and her outlook was amazing.

May 16

My only hope is in your love and faithfulness.   PSALM 40:11

August 17

Because of our faith, He has brought us into this place of highest privilege.   ROMANS 5:2

May 17

She wouldn't give up her favorite pair of jeans, her passion for God, or her determination to show the world how one-of-a-kind she is.

August 16

*I*s that a joyous choir I hear? No, it is the Lord Himself exulting over you in happy song.   ZEPHANIAH 3:18

May 18

𝒴our workmanship is marvelous—and how well I know it.

PSALM 139:14

August 15

Aren't you tickled pink to be the joy of God's heart... the reason for His happy song?

May 19

When we give our all to God, He makes all things beautiful.

August 14

Kind words are like honey—enjoyable and healthful.

PROVERBS 16:24

May 20

Give yourselves humbly to god. JAMES 4:7

August 13

Love forgets mistakes. **PROVERBS 17:9**

May 21

When you draw close to God, God will draw close to you.

JAMES 4:8

August 12

Remember the good–let go of the rest!

May 22

God's plan for your life is as special as you are.

August 11

*Y*our spiritual strength comes as a gift from god. HEBREWS 13:9

May 23

*Y*ou both precede and follow me, and place your hand of blessing on my head. PSALM 139:5

August 10

Look after each other so that not one of you will fail to find God's best blessings.   HEBREWS 12:15

May 24

*E*very girl needs a cute purse, red shoes, and a good place to be alone with God.

August 9

A little black dress, a great hair style, a flattering pair of heels—just some of the things that make you feel like the fabulous woman God created you to be!

May 25

*L*et us go right in, to God Himself, with true hearts fully trusting Him to receive us.   HEBREWS 10:22

August 8

*G*od blesses those who are kind. PSALM 41:1

May 26

The one thing I want from God, the thing I seek most of all,
is the privilege of... living in His presence every day of my life.

PSALM 27:4

August 7

If God cares so wonderfully for flowers... won't He more surely care for you?   MATTHEW 6:30

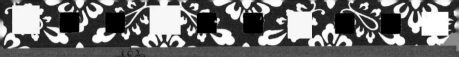

May 27

Girlfriends are an essential part of God's goodness to us.

August 6

Make your life like a garden full of daisies...
bright and happy to be basking in the Lord's care.

May 28

Whatever is good and perfect comes to us from God.   JAMES 1:17

August 5

You have been with me from birth and have helped me constantly—no wonder I am always praising you! PSALM 71:6

May 29

Chocolate is proof that God is sensitive to our needs...
and meets each one perfectly.

August 4

I will tell everyone how good you are, and of your constant, daily care. PSALM 71:15

May 30

*M*any blessings are given to those who trust the Lord.   PSALM 40:4

August 3

The shoes matched her dress perfectly, and she smiled, knowing God had put her day together with the same attention to detail.

May 31

*Y*our goodness and unfailing kindness shall be with me all of my life.

PSALM 23:6

August 2

We are able to hold our heads high no matter what happens and know that all is well, for we know how dearly God loves us.

ROMANS 5:5

June 1

Faith is having the courage to believe God will do it before we see it.

August 1

Let your conversation be gracious as well as sensible.

COLOSSIANS 4:6

June 2

𝒲hat we hope for is waiting for us, even though
we cannot see it up ahead.   HEBREWS 11:1

July 31

Let the spirit of god empower you to face every challenge with style and grace.

June 3

She was brave on the inside, where God does great things...
and that's what mattered most.

July 30

Be gentle and ready to forgive.   COLOSSIANS 3:13

June 4

How we thank god for all of this! it is He who makes us victorious through jesus.   I CORINTHIANS 15:57

July 29

*P*ut on gentleness like a favorite summer dress...
let it be an easy and comfortable part of your life.

June 5

$\mathscr{I}$f you will stir up this inner power, you will never be afraid.

II TIMOTHY 1:8

July 28

Create in me a new, clean heart, o god.   PSALM 51:10

June 6

*T*here's a certain loveliness in the woman who's in love with god.

July 27

I am radiant with joy because of your mercy. PSALM 31:7

June 7

Praise her for the many fine things she does. These good deeds of hers shall bring her honor. PROVERBS 31:31

July 26

*Glimpse at the beauty around you today—
it's nothing compared to the beauty within you.*

June 8

*P*ractice tenderhearted mercy and kindness to others.

COLOSSIANS 3:12

July 25

*Y*ou chart the path ahead of me, and tell me where to stop and rest.   PSALM 139:3

June 9

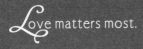
Love matters most.

July 24

How precious it is, Lord, to realize that You are thinking about me constantly! PSALM 139:17

June 10

In response to all He has done for us, let us outdo each other in being helpful and kind.   HEBREWS 10:24

July 23

A little pampering does a girl good—
you are delicately made and precious to your Maker.

June 11

God has a plan for you today—and it's good in every way.

July 22

Live one day at a time.   MATTHEW 6:34

June 12

O Lord, my god... we are ever in your thoughts.   PSALM 40:5

July 21

*D*on't be anxious about tomorrow. God will take care of your tomorrow too.   MATTHEW 6:34

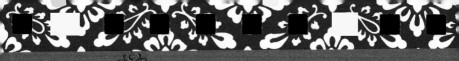

June 13

The Lord's blessing is our greatest wealth.   PROVERBS 10:22

July 20

Today is God's gift to you—shine!

June 14

𝒢od paints every flower a beautiful hue...
and your life with a beautiful purpose.

July 19

Don't be afraid, for the Lord will go before you and will
be with you; He will not fail you.   DEUTERONOMY 31:8

June 15

*H*e fulfills the desires of those who reverence and trust HIM.

PSALM 145:19

July 18

*F*ace your day with a new sense of confidence—God is with you!

June 16

*I*t is a wonderful thing to be alive! ECCLESIASTES 11:7

July 17

*T*hose who turn many to righteousness will glitter like the stars forever.   DANIEL 12:3

June 17

She had a spring in her step, god on her side, and a fearless heart to face the day.

July 16

*L*et your favor shine again upon your servant.   PSALM 31:16

June 18

When the path ahead of us is washed away,
God will give us wings.

July 15

The graceful beauty of God shined on her... as if she strolled through her day under a spotlight from heaven.

June 19

*O*nly god can see everything. ECCLESIASTES 8:17

July 14

Let everything He has made give praise to Him.   PSALM 148:5

June 20

The Lord is faithful to His promises. Blessed are all those who wait for Him to help them.   ISAIAH 30:18

July 13

Head to toe, you're exquisitely made.

June 21

$\mathcal{F}$rom a broken heel to a broken heart—God cares.

July 12

*Y*ou want to be tools in the hands of God, to be used for HIS good purposes.   ROMANS 6:13

June 22

The Lord still waits for you to come to Him, so He can show you his love. ISAIAH 30:18

July 11

*E*very elegant detail of who you are was designed
for the purposes of God.

June 23

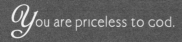 You are priceless to god.

July 10

Give him first place in your life and live as he wants you to.

MATTHEW 6:33

June 24

$\mathcal{G}$od has given you something you can give back to the world—
in a way no one else can.

July 9

I chose you! I appointed you to go and produce lovely fruit.

JOHN 15:16

June 25

The godly are able to be generous with their gifts.   PSALM 37:26

July 8

*I*n God's eyes you are loved, and you are lovely.

June 26

Give generously, for your gifts will return to you later.

ECCLESIASTES 11:1

July 7

𝒟on't hide your light! Let it shine for all. MATTHEW 5:15

June 27

Sand between your toes... ocean breeze... blue sky...

glorious gifts from a generous God.

July 6

Shine your god-given light on those around you today.

June 28

The earth belongs to god! Everything in all the world is his!

PSALM 24:1

July 5

God gives those who please HIM wisdom, knowledge, and joy.

ECCLESIASTES 2:25

June 29

The heavens are telling the glory of God; they are a marvelous display of His craftsmanship.   PSALM 19:1

July 4

Live with joy!

June 30

Lord, make me all you want me to be!

July 3

$\mathcal{W}$e confidently and joyfully look forward to actually becoming all that God has had in mind for us to be.   ROMANS 5:2

July 1

Stir into flame the strength and boldness that is in you.

II TIMOTHY 1:6

July 2

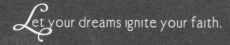

Let your dreams ignite your faith.